The Twits

by Roald Dahl
Adapted for the stage by David Wood

Samuel French — London
New York - Toronto - Hollywood

It is a condition of the issue of a performing licence for this play that the names of David Wood and Roald Dahl should appear in print of equal size and prominence and that the one is never mentioned without the other on all programmes and publicity material for productions.

THE TWITS

The Twits was commissioned by the Belgrade Theatre, Coventry, and first performed there on 25th March, 1999, with the following cast:

Mr Twit	Andy Hockley
Mrs Twit	Isabel Ford
Mr Muggle-Wump	Anthony Ofoegbu
Mrs Muggle-Wump	Rachael Savage
Roly-Poly Bird	Jenny Sanderson
Narrator	David Baker
Children	Sophie Gabel, Lucy Haines,

Jason Harvey, Gary Hornsby, Kelly Hynes,
Lisa Kelly, Shazeer Mahmood, Sophie Majrowski,
Sabrina Moustakim, Stephanie Nicely,
Luka Owen and Alexander Smith

Producer **Jane Hytch**
Director **Kathi Leahy**
Assistant Director **Kay Fellows**
Designer **Tom Conroy**
Lighting Designer **Wesley Hiscock**
Choreography by **Jill Freeman** and **Kathi Leahy**

CHARACTERS

Mr Twit
Mrs Twit
The Muggle-Wump Family—monkeys:
Muggle-Wump (Dad)
Mrs Muggle-Wump (Mum)
Little Muggle-Wump 1
Little Muggle-Wump 2
Little Muggle-Wump 3
The Roly-Poly Bird (male or female)
Birds (it is suggested that these are puppets on rods, carried by children, who could also be dressed as birds)
Monkeys (optional—other monkeys living in the rain forest, perhaps played by children)
Narrator/Musician (individual productions may decide to have other musicians too, but the idea of the Narrator "accompanying" the action with percussion or other instruments works well)

Acknowledgements

David Wood would like to thank Bob Eaton and Jane Hytch of the Belgrade Theatre, Coventry, for commissioning this play, and Kathi Leahy for directing such a splendid production.

———————————

The cover illustration of The Twits, by Quentin Blake, is reproduced by permission of A.P. Watt Ltd, 20 John Street, London, WC1N 2DR, and the artist.

———————————

Samuel French Ltd acknowledges the publication of the original book by the late Roald Dahl by Jonathan Cape Limited in hardback format and Puffin Books in paperback format.

PRODUCTION NOTES

Most of the cast need to be physical performers. The Muggle-Wump family should all be fairly acrobatic. It is possible that the Roly-Poly Bird should be able to fly on a trapeze. Mrs Twit will have to be flown on a rope. Mr Twit will need to be agile, particularly when he glues the branches of the tree.

The Narrator/Musician links the story. He could be a multi-instrumentalist, complete with mad percussion kit noises as well as keyboard, who can also project as an outgoing presenter.

There could be several Birds on each rod, so that four or five children can create quite a flock! They should be different colours and sizes, fantasy birds rather than realistic English garden birds, which might look rather drab. But they should not prove any competition for the Roly-Poly Bird, who should be flamboyant and brightly coloured. Two rods carry black birds (one on each rod) holding paintbrushes in their beaks.

Concept
The challenge, as I see it, of adapting this book is that many of the episodes are so "gross" that to play them for real would probably not be as effective as playing them in a stylised up-front, presentational manner. The fact that the book tells us that Mr and Mrs Twit once trained monkeys in a circus suggested the idea of setting the whole play within a circus ring. This means that certain key episodes can be played almost as circus acts.

However, there is a danger in this. It would be wrong to make light of the unpleasantness and cruelty of the Twits, because we must get our children's audience well and truly on the side of the animals. There will be many times when we want to play for a more convincing sense of danger than in, for instance, the often winking, conspiratorial (with the audience) comedy-style performance often given by villains in pantomime. We have to find the right balance.

The use of our Narrator as a linking device will hopefully have echoes of the role of a circus ringmaster, taking us from one act to the next; if necessary, setting the scene and filling in certain elements of the story which would otherwise be difficult to stage.

It is also worth mentioning that the circus style will be imposed upon a through story-line, which must be preserved; the play mustn't appear to be just a series of turns. But hopefully we can get the best of both worlds—the excitement of the circus, coupled with the dramatic momentum of a story enacted with a combination of "truth" and "big" acting.

The more physical skills that can be incorporated into the production the better.

Set

A circus ring, with access from the sides and possibly the back. The Narrator/ Musician must be on stage. He will need to be able to roam, but never be too far away from his instruments, which will often punctuate as well as follow his announcements and links. The original production gave him an enormous tricycle to ride round on.

There are three main large set pieces, which ideally will be on trucks. They should not be visible at the beginning of the play, but will be brought in at various points in Act I. (NB: the original production successfully kept the caravan and the tree on stage from the very beginning; only the cage "entered" during the action.)

The set pieces are:

The Twits' caravan. Ideally this will be able to revolve or open up at the front, revealing their living accommodation. In Act II, the whole of the interior needs to revolve (not necessarily in vision), so that we can see the room upside down. Hopefully the caravan will be large enough for the Twits to stand inside it. However, individual scenes at, for example, their dining table, can be played outside the caravan, further down in the circus ring acting area.

The Muggle-Wump family's cage. This need not be too big, as long as there is room for the monkeys to all stand and sit together, as well as stand on top of one another, so the height should accommodate this. A door, with a large key, gives access.

The Tree. In the book this is called the Big Dead Tree, and it certainly could be a skeletal structure with branches on which the puppet Birds will "sit".

All three sets need to be on stage at the same time. I am imagining the caravan in the middle, with the cage to one side and the tree to the other side. Once all three are in position, it is quite likely they will stay there for most of the action of the play.

Bearing in mind that we will need the actors to climb on top of the cage and the tree (Mr Twit puts glue on them, and it may also be fun to have the monkeys climb on them), it is important that they can be made safe and strong enough to accommodate such activity.

I have also introduced two scenes set in the African rainforest. These will occur when the other three set pieces need not be on stage. The rainforest setting could be created very simply with ropes made to look like vines or whatever those things are that Tarzan swings on! Maybe some greenery flown in too? And, if the Roly-Poly Bird can work on a trapeze, it could be useful here. However, the rainforest scenes are not intended to be lengthy, and we must be able to move to and from them with the minimum of delay.

Towards the end of the play, Mrs Twit has to be lifted up in the air by masses of balloons. Obviously some sort of flying device will be necessary for this. It might be visually effective if our basic circus ring set incorporates several bunches of balloons filled with helium, at various points around the ring. These can then be used for the flying sequence.

Costume
Presumably it is best to follow the guidelines given by Quentin Blake's illustrations in the book. However, it may be thought necessary to give the Twits something a bit more glittery, for their first appearance. Whether or not they should look like clowns, I'm not sure. That is what they are, in many ways, but they should be revolting, not glamorous!

The Muggle-Wumps need to be able to move well, so their costumes will probably be quite simple. However, they must be endearingly woolly—I don't think simple brown leotards will do! They should probably have a close-fitting helmet-style of head-dress, leaving their faces free to be made up. Obviously they must have full vision.

The children carrying the Birds could be dressed like birds themselves or wear a basic circus costume. But they shouldn't look too bright, as the focus must be on the puppet Birds.

The Roly-Poly Bird should be very exotic, but he/she will need as much freedom of movement as possible.

The Narrator shouldn't look like a conventional ringmaster. He could wear a colourful shirt and waistcoat, and a fun version of a top hat.

DW

OTHER PLAYS AND MUSICALS BY DAVID WOOD

Aladdin
The BFG (based on the book by Roald Dahl)
Babe, the Sheep-Pig (based on the book by Dick King-Smith)
Babes in the Magic Wood
Cinderella
Dick Whittington and Wondercat
Dinosaurs and all that Rubbish (based on the book by Michael Foreman)
Flibberty and the Penguin
The Gingerbread Man
Hijack Over Hygenia
The Ideal Gnome Expedition
Jack and the Giant
Jack the Lad (co-written with Dave and Toni Arthur)
Larry the Lamb in Toytown (co-written with Sheila Ruskin, adapted from
the stories of S.G. Hulme-Beaman)
Meg and Mog Show (from the books by Helen Nicoll
and Jan Pieńkowski)
More Adventures of Noddy (based on the stories by Enid Blyton)
Mother Goose's Golden Christmas
Noddy (based on the stories by Enid Blyton)
Nutcracker Sweet
Old Father Time
The Old Man of Lochnagar (based on the book by HRH The Prince of
Wales)
Old Mother Hubbard
The Owl and the Pussycat went to See... (co-written with Sheila Ruskin)
The Papertown Paperchase
The Pied Piper (co-written with Dave and Toni Arthur)
The Plotters of Cabbage Patch Corner
Robin Hood (co-written with Dave and Toni Arthur)
Rupert and the Green Dragon (based on the Rupert stories and characters
by Mary Tourtel and Alfred Bestall)
Save the Human (based on the story by Tony Husband and David Wood)
The See-Saw Tree
The Selfish Shellfish
There Was An Old Woman...
Tickle (one act)
The Witches (based on the book by Roald Dahl)

Theatre for Children—Guide to Writing, Adapting, Directing and Acting
(written with Janet Grant, published by Faber and Faber)

ACT I

Before the play begins, perhaps circus-style music plays, live or recorded, to set a jolly atmosphere

As the House Lights fade, an overture, quirky and fun, with lots of percussion, is played. Ideally the musician/s is/are on stage. Fanfare/drumroll

The Narrator, possibly a musician, steps forward

Narrator Ladies and gentlemen, young ladies and gentlemen, the Belgrade (*or local town*) Super Circus is proud to present an exciting, extraordinary extravaganza entittle-i-titled... *The Twits*, featuring first the funny, fantastically fit, mirthful monarchs of monkeydom—please put your hands together for the Muggle-Wumps!

Music as the Muggle-Wump Family enter and perform a short, impressive but not too impressive, acrobatic routine

Applause as the Muggle-Wumps exit, or stay on to see the other acts

Now please welcome, in a fabulous formation of feathered flight, the Belgrade Super Circus' Fantasy of Birds!

Music as the Birds enter and show off their skills. Perhaps the puppet birds are in colourful UV

Applause as the Birds exit, or stay on to see the other acts

Next, my friends, prepare to meet our special guest star, straight from the magical, exotic, African rainforest, the clever, colourful, charismatic Roly-Poly Bird!

The Roly-Poly Bird makes a spectacular entrance, possibly flying high to show off his rainbow-coloured plumage

Applause as the Roly-Poly Bird exits, or stays on to watch the final act

It's time to meet and greet the stars of our show. Be prepared. They're

shocking, they're silly, they're stupid, they're stupifyingly soppy, they're—
get ready for—the one and only—thank goodness—the Twits!

The Twits enter, wearing spangly cloaks. Mrs Twit carries a walking stick

*Music as they perform a short comedy routine, silent not spoken. Perhaps Mr
Twit presents, in an extravagant display of chivalry, a bouquet to Mrs Twit.
She reacts delighted. She sniffs the flowers, which wilt or fall off. Mr Twit
laughs. Mrs Twit hits him. Mr Twit reacts by falling. His false teeth come out
and he holds them as they chatter. He politely offers a chair to Mrs Twit. As
she sits, he puts the teeth under her. She reacts as though bitten and rubs her
bottom. Mr Twit laughs and retrieves the teeth. He goes to sit, but Mrs Twit
pulls the chair from under him. He crashes to the floor, reacts and rubs his
bottom. Mrs Twit goes to sit and Mr Twit kicks the chair away. Mrs Twit
crashes to the floor. This act can be worked on in rehearsal and changed or
developed as required. But it should not be too "domestic" or feature food,
because it should not pre-empt any of the "home-life" incidents that occur
later*

Applause as the Twits take their bow

*Music as the scene changes. The other characters, if they have stayed on,
now exit*

*The Twits, if necessary helped by stage management (as circus staff), bring
on their caravan and park it* UC *of the ring*

As they do so, the Narrator comes forward. He leads us into the story proper

Ladies and gents, young ladies, young gents. Our story begins away from
the glamour of the circus. Far, far away.

*Mr and Mrs Twit remove their spangly costumes, revealing their drab,
dirty, everyday clothes*

*They leave their circus costumes with the caravan and come forward into the
ring, acting out the Narrator's words*

The Twits lived in a caravan. The best word to describe them was ...
disgusting. Mr Twit...

Mr Twit steps forward

...was a very hairy-faced man. His thick, spiky hair stuck out straight like the bristles of a nailbrush. The stuff even sprouted in revolting tufts out of his nostrils and ear-holes.

Mr Twit My hairiness…

Narrator …thought Mr Twit…

Mr Twit …makes me look terrifically wise and grand!

Narrator But in truth he was neither of these things. Mr Twit was a twit. He was born a twit.

Mrs Twit (*coming forward*) And now, at the age of sixty, he's a bigger twit than ever!

Mr Twit looks daggers at Mrs Twit

Narrator How often, you may ask, did Mr Twit wash this bristly, nailbrushy face of his? The answer is *never*.

Mr Twit (*proudly*) Not even on Sundays!

Narrator As a result, there were always hundreds of bits of old breakfasts and lunches and suppers sticking to the hairs.

Mr Twit licks eagerly round his face

Specks of gravy, dried-up scrambled egg, spinach, tomato ketchup, fish fingers…

Mr Twit (*with relish*) …minced chicken livers!

Narrator If you delved deeper still—hold your noses, ladies and gentlemen—you'd discover things that had been there for months and months.

Mr Twit delves and finds…

Mr Twit A piece of maggoty green cheese! (*He eats it noisily*)

Narrator A mouldy old cornflake!

Mr Twit finds it and eats it

Or even…

Mr Twit (*digging it out*) …the slimy tail of a tinned sardine. (*He holds it aloft*)

Mrs Twit grabs it and eats it with relish

Mrs Twit Mmmm. Tasty.

Mr Twit looks daggers at her

Narrator Mrs Twit was no better than her husband.

Mr Twit You ... you ugly old hag!

Mrs Twit reacts

Narrator Ugly, yes. But not born ugly. When she was young she had quite
a pretty face.

Mrs Twit smiles "prettily"

But she had ugly thoughts every day of every week of every year, and so
her face got uglier...
Mr Twit ...and uglier...
Narrator ...and uglier...

Mrs Twit demonstrates

Mr Twit ...so ugly I can hardly bear to look at it!

Mrs Twit looks daggers at Mr Twit. Then she hits him with her walking stick

Ow! (*He holds his arm up threateningly*)

Both freeze

Narrator Mr and Mrs Twit were a very happy couple. But seldom happy at
the same time. For what really made them happy was playing nasty tricks
on one another...

*Music as, unseen by Mrs Twit, Mr Twit snaps off the lower half of her walking
stick. Then he goes to the caravan and sits at the table, pouring out two
glasses of beer*

Mr Twit (*warmly*) A glass of beer, my dear?

Mrs Twit unfreezes

Mrs Twit Mmmm. Lovely. (*She goes to walk, using her stick, but it is so
short she crashes to the floor*)

Mr Twit laughs

Aaaah! (*She struggles up, forced to stoop because of the short walking
stick*) What's happened?

Mr Twit quickly removes his shoes, kneels down into them and shuffles towards her

Mr Twit You seem to be growing, my sweet.
Mrs Twit Growing?
Mr Twit (*arriving, and looking shorter than her*) Growing. Take a look at your stick, you old goat, and see how much you've grown in comparison.
Mrs Twit (*looking at her stick, in amazement*) Never!
Mr Twit You always said you wanted me to look up to you! Your wish has been granted.
Mrs Twit I don't want to grow!
Mr Twit No?
Mrs Twit No! Do something!
Mr Twit Do something? Anything?
Mrs Twit Anything! Stop me growing!
Mr Twit Of course, my pet.

Mr Twit stands up, unseen by Mrs Twit, and fetches an enormous joke mallet, which he brings crashing down on her head

Mrs Twit Aaah!

Mr Twit laughs and, seen by Mrs Twit, replaces the bottom half of her walking stick

Mr Twit Just a little joke, my honey-bunny!

Mrs Twit growls in fury. Both go to sit at the table and drink their beer. Mr Twit belches

Narrator Mrs Twit was determined to pay back Mr Twit.

Musical sting. Mrs Twit smiles

Suddenly she had an idea.

Mrs Twit checks Mr Twit is not looking

Into her beer she dropped...

Mrs Twit follows the narration

...her glass eye...

Music as Mr Twit looks round with a hint of suspicion. Mrs Twit smiles innocently. Mr Twit drinks from his glass. Mrs Twit pretends to drink from hers. Then she pretends to notice something behind Mr Twit. He turns to follow her gaze. Quickly, Mrs Twit swaps round the two glasses. Mr Twit turns back, suspicious. Mrs Twit drinks from his glass, he drinks from hers

Mr Twit What are you plotting?
Mrs Twit Me plotting? You're the rotter what plots. But I'm watching you. Oh yes! (*Smugly she turns briefly away*)

Mr Twit quickly swaps round the glasses. Mrs Twit turns back, suspicious. Mr Twit drinks. Mrs Twit drinks, unsure of which glass she has. Mr Twit suddenly starts to sneeze

Mr Twit Ah, ah, ah… (*He looks for a hanky but can't find one*) …tishoo!

While Mr Twit holds up his beard, sneezes into it, then wipes his nose on his sleeves, Mrs Twit quickly swaps round the glasses again. Mr Twit picks up his glass—in fact her glass—and starts to drink. The music builds

Mrs Twit Oh yes, I'm watching you like a wombat!
Mr Twit (*spraying her with beer as he talks*) Oh, do shut up, you old hag. (*He drains the glass and suddenly sees the glass eye at the bottom. He jumps with shock*) Aaaah!

Mrs Twit cackles with laughter

Mrs Twit I told you I was watching you! I've got eyes everywhere, so you'd better be careful! (*She retrieves the glass eye from the glass and holds it towards Mr Twit, meaningfully, then replaces it in her eye-socket*)

The Narrator comes forward

Narrator One day, Mr Twit announced…
Mr Twit I've been thinking.
Mrs Twit Did it hurt?
Mr Twit I am going…
Mrs Twit The further the better!
Mr Twit I am going to run a circus!
Mrs Twit To what, you twit?
Mr Twit To run a circus!
Mrs Twit Run a circus? You couldn't run an egg and spoon race.
Mr Twit You wait, you old trout. (*Grandly*) I will train animals.

Mrs Twit Animals, what animals?
Mr Twit (*after a pause for thought*) Monkeys!
Mrs Twit Monkeys? Where will you find monkeys?
Mr Twit In the rainforests of deepest, darkest Africa!

Immediately, the Lighting changes and evocative music plays. Ropes like vines drop. We are in the rainforest

The Twits exit

The Muggle-Wump family enter and—optionally—other monkeys

They play happily, climbing ropes and chasing one another. (In the original production, Mr and Mrs Muggle-Wump entered separately, then, while the other monkeys played, met up with their children and established themselves as a family unit)

After a while, in flies the Roly-Poly Bird

Roly-Poly Bird Wheeeeeeeee!
Muggle-Wump It's the Roly-Poly Bird!
Mrs Muggle-Wump Look, children, the Roly-Poly Bird!

The Muggle-Wumps look up

Roly-Poly Bird Morning, Muggle-Wump! Morning, Mrs Muggle-Wump! Morning, little Muggle-Wumps!
Muggle-Wumps Morning, Roly-Poly Bird!
Roly-Poly Bird What a marvellous, magical morning!

The Roly-Poly Bird flies impressively, watched by the admiring Muggle-Wumps

Muggle-Wumps Oooh! Aaaah! Wheee!

Unseen by the Muggle-Wumps, Mr Twit, in an explorer's hat, enters. He sees the Muggle-Wumps and rubs his hands in glee

The Roly-Poly Bird finishes his display. Mr Twit produces a banana and half unpeels it. He holds it out, then starts behaving like a monkey. A Little Muggle-Wump sees him. Tension music as Mr Twit tempts him with the banana. The Little Muggle-Wump advances. The others notice and react alarmed. Perhaps the audience shout a warning. But the Little Muggle-

Wump goes closer and closer and nibbles the banana. It tastes good. Mr Twit starts to dance a monkey dance. Jungle rhythms start. The Little Muggle-Wump happily joins in. One by one, all the Muggle-Wumps approach and join in too. They dance happily, as if in a trance, circling Mr Twit. The Roly-Poly Bird watches. The dance builds in intensity. Suddenly Mr Twit slips out of the circle, leaving the Muggle-Wumps happily prancing. Then Mr Twit catches them all in a large net. (He either uses a huge butterfly net or releases a net from above, then tightens it.) The Muggle-Wumps are trapped. They squeal and screech. The other (optional) monkeys react in fright and hide. The Roly-Poly Bird is concerned and flies towards Mr Twit, who pushes him off. NB: in the original production Mr Twit captured the Little Muggle-Wump, unseen by the others, and led him off. He then returned with a large loudspeaker; he turned a knob and Little Muggle-Wump's cries for help echoed out. The remaining Muggle-Wumps approached the loudspeaker, concerned. Then Mr Twit caught them all in a net

Mr Twit Got you, my lovelies! You're mine, all mine! You're coming with me. To England! (*He starts to drag the Muggle-Wumps away*)

The other (optional) monkeys emerge and watch and sadly wave

Muggle-Wumps (*calling for help*) Roly-Poly Bird! Roly-Poly Bird!
Roly-Poly Bird   (*calling after them*) Be brave, Muggle-Wumps!
                                          Tails up, heads high!
                                          Come the spring, to you I'll fly!
                                          Till then, goodbye my friends, goodby—e!

The Roly-Poly Bird flies off

Mr Twit drags the netted Muggle-Wumps round the "ring" till they arrive back in England

Narrator Back in England, the Twits prepared the Muggle-Wumps for work.

Music as Mrs Twit joins Mr Twit

They remove the net and the Muggle-Wumps cower in a clump. Each is pulled from the group to be dressed in a simple costume—a tutu or a bolero jacket or a hat. They are totally dejected. NB: this sequence should not take too long, and ideally should be mimed. However, if Mr and Mrs Twit need lines to cover the dressing-up of the Muggle-Wumps, they should use brief commands or exhortations, a mixture of uncompromising harshness and twee, patronising praise. For example:

Mr and Mrs Twit	Arms up! Arms in! Pretty monkey!
	Stay still! Turn round! In! On!
	Clever, clever! That's it, my lovely!
	What a good monkey!
	Don't move till I tell you!
	Up! Turn! Arm! Leg!
	Handsome as a human. Nearly.
	Don't you look sweety-weety, cutesy-wutesy!
	Aaah! Pretty little monkey-person.

Then Mr Twit tries to force them to perform. He uses Mrs Twit's stick to prod them into rolling head over heels or jump in the air. They resist. They poke out their tongues and cock snooks at Mr Twit, who grows increasingly frustrated and cross. This sequence, too, should not be too long and should ideally be mimed. But if Mr Twit needs the occasional line, it should be a short, sharp instruction. For example: "Up! Down! Stay! Over! Jump! Back! Roll! Go! Turn!" No more should be necessary at this stage of their training. Mrs Twit watches, unimpressed, scorning Mr Twit's efforts. Finally the Twits pull on a large cage one side of the stage, and force the Muggle-Wumps to enter it. Mr Twit locks it with a large key. The Twits return to their caravan as the Lighting fades to night-time. Moonlight illuminates the cage. The Muggle-Wumps are huddled up inside

Little Muggle-Wump 1 Mum?
Mrs Muggle-Wump Yes, dear?
Little Muggle-Wump 1 This place stinks.
Mrs Muggle-Wump Yes, dear. Go to sleep.

Pause

Little Muggle-Wump 2 Dad?
Muggle-Wump Yes, son?
Little Muggle-Wump 2 I want to go home.
Muggle-Wump We'd all like to go home, son. Go to sleep.

Pause

Little Muggle-Wump 3 Mum?
Mrs Muggle-Wump Yes, dear?
Little Muggle-Wump 3 I'm cold.
Mrs Muggle-Wump Cuddle up to me and go to sleep.

Pause

Little Muggle-Wump 1 Dad?
Muggle-Wump Yes?
Little Muggle-Wump 1 Tell us a story.
Muggle-Wump Well…
Little Muggle-Wumps Please!
Muggle-Wump All right. Once upon a time there was a friendly forest in a beautiful far-off land. In the tall, sweet-smelling trees a family of monkeys played, and every day their friend the Roly-Poly Bird came to say hallo. And they were all happy.

Pause

Little Muggle-Wump 1 Is that it?
Muggle-Wump That's it.
Little Muggle-Wump 1 (*with a yawn*) It's a nice story.

The Muggle-Wumps settle to sleep. The Lighting fades on the cage. Music as the Lighting comes up on the caravan, where Mr and Mrs Twit prepare for bed. They undress, revealing funny night attire. Then they get into bed

Mrs Twit Them blooming monkeys are a waste of space.
Mr Twit Shut up, fungus face.
Mrs Twit A load of woolly wallies, that's all they are.
Mr Twit That's all you know, camel-breath.
Mrs Twit All I know is you'll never train them chattering charlies.
Mr Twit Yes, I will!
Mrs Twit No, you won't!
Mr Twit I will!
Mrs Twit You won't!
Mr Twit Will!
Mrs Twit Won't!
Mr Twit Will!
Mrs Twit Won't!
Mr Twit Won't!
Mrs Twit Will!
Mr Twit Hah! Gotcha! (*He gets out of bed*)
Mrs Twit Where are you off to?
Mr Twit I want a drink.
Mrs Twit You want a brain. (*She laughs heartily, then dozes off, snoring gently*)

The Narrator comes forward as Mr Twit gets a glass of water. He puts it down as an idea strikes him

Narrator Mr Twit hadn't forgotten his wife's glass eye trick. He decided to pay her back.

Music as Mr Twit reaches into his beard and brings out a large, slimy frog. Alternatively he goes "outside" and finds it

Mr Twit Come on, fat froggy, do your slimy, grimy worst! (*Smiling in anticipation, he slips it under the sheet at the foot of the bed*)

Pause. Mr Twit watches as the shape of the frog moves under the sheet

Mrs Twit Aaaaaaah! (*She bounces about*)
Mr Twit What's the matter, light of my life?
Mrs Twit Help! There's something in the bed!
Mr Twit I'll bet it's that Giant Skillywiggler!
Mrs Twit What Skigglewilly? Ah! It's all slimy!
Mr Twit The Giant Skillywiggler that jumped out of my suitcase when I got home from Africa.
Mrs Twit Never!
Mr Twit Yes. I tried to kill it, but it got away. It disappeared under a pile of your knickers!
Mrs Twit Help! Save me! It's crawling on my feet!
Mr Twit It's got teeth like screwdrivers.
Mrs Twit Aaaah!
Mr Twit It'll bite off your toes!
Mrs Twit Aaaah!
Mr Twit And nibble your knees!
Mrs Twit Aaaaaaaah! It's tickling my tummy!

Mr Twit pulls back the sheet. The frog jumps up on to Mrs Twit's face

My nose! My nose!

Mr Twit grabs the frog and holds it up

Mr Twit By golly it *is* a Giant Skillywiggler!
Mrs Twit Aaaahh! (*She faints*)

Mr Twit laughs heartily, then throws the glass of water in Mrs Twit's face. She wakes with a splutter, then chases Mr Twit off

You scabby old scumbag!
You sneaky old snake!

You scheming old scallop!
You wait! You wait!

Lights up on the Narrator

Narrator Near the Twits' caravan stood the Big Dead Tree.

Music as the tree enters. It stands on the side of the stage opposite the cage

Every evening, as the sun went down, birds would fly in from all around to roost for the night on its branches.

Music as the Birds enter

A short, visually magical sequence follows, as the birds fly in formation around the stage

On one particular evening, as the Muggle-Wumps relaxed after a hard day's training...

The Muggle-Wumps stir in the cage

Little Muggle-Wump 1 Hey, Mum, Dad!
Little Muggle-Wump 2 Look!
Little Muggle-Wump 3 Look at the birds!

The Muggle-Wumps watch. Eventually the Birds land and settle on the branches of the tree

Mr and Mrs Twit enter with a bowl of food

Mr Twit Come and get it, my lovelies. Grub up! (*He opens the cage with the key and pushes in the bowl*)

The Muggle-Wumps press round and start feeding

Mrs Twit They're eating us out of house and home, them greedy guzzlers.
Mr Twit Got to feed 'em up. Build up their strength. They'll never perform on empty stomachs.
Mrs Twit They'll never perform full stop. Mangy mugginses. (*She prods them with her stick. To the Muggle-Wumps*) That's my supper you're stuffing!
Mr Twit Shut up moaning. Come the day they make us rich and famous you'll have caviar and champagne.

Mrs Twit If I haven't starved to death in the meantime. (*She sees the Birds*)
   Oh look, the blooming birds are back. I hate them, messy creatures. (*She
   advances with her stick*) Clear off...
Mr Twit (*stopping her*) Wait, wait! (*He points at the Birds*) Supper!
Mrs Twit Eh?
Mr Twit Tasty, toothsome, tickle your palate... Bird Pie!

Mrs Twit's eyes light up

   Shhhh!

*Mr and Mrs Twit creep backwards, not wanting to disturb the birds, then
vanish behind the caravan. The Muggle-Wumps watch them as they go*

Little Muggle-Wump 1 Mum!
Little Muggle-Wump 2 Dad!
Little Muggle-Wump 3 What's going on?
Mrs Muggle-Wump Shh! Something to do with the birds.
Little Muggle-Wump 1 Don't they like them?
Muggle-Wump Oh yes, son. I think they like them a lot...

*Music as the Twits enter with a large net on a long pole. They gingerly
approach the tree*

Mr Twit (*grabbing the net*) I'll do it!
Mrs Twit (*grabbing the net*) I'll do it!
Mr Twit (*grabbing the net*) I'll do it!
Mrs Twit (*grabbing the net*) I'll do it!
Mr Twit ⎫
           ⎬ (*together*) Oh, all right, then. *You* do it.
Mrs Twit ⎭

They drop the net with a clatter. The birds stir, but settle again

Mr Twit ⎫
           ⎬ (*together*) Shhh!
Mrs Twit ⎭

Mr Twit grabs the net and slowly advances. Mrs Twit pushes him

Mrs Twit Go on.
Mr Twit Shut up! (*He turns, swinging the net, hitting Mrs Twit*)
Mrs Twit Ow!
Mr Twit Shut up! (*He swings back. The net hits Mrs Twit again*)
Mrs Twit Ow!
Mr Twit Shhh!

They start off again

   (*Suddenly*) Now! (*He swings the net back over his head, "catching" Mrs Twit*)

She thrashes around inside. They sort themselves out. They advance again, nearer and nearer

   (*Suddenly*) Charge! (*He trips over the net, which clatters to the ground*)

   The Birds fly away and exit

The Muggle-Wumps happily applaud. Mr Twit looks meaningfully at them. They stop and settle. Mrs Twit laughs

   You clumsy warthog!
Mrs Twit Clumsy yourself!
Mr Twit It was your fault!
Mrs Twit It wasn't my fault!
Mr Twit It was!
Mrs Twit It wasn't!
Mr Twit Was!
Mrs Twit Wasn't, wasn't, wasn't!

They freeze, looking daggers at each other. The Narrator steps in

Narrator Mrs Twit hadn't forgotten about her husband's Giant Skillywiggler joke. She decided to pay him back.

The Twits unfreeze

Mrs Twit (*charmingly*) Never mind about the Bird Pie, my dearest. We can try again tomorrow.
Mr Twit Mmm.
Mrs Twit Why don't I make us each a nice, mouth-watering bowl of spaghetti instead. Eh?
Mr Twit Mm. Yes. Why not, my little dumpling? Good idea. Spaghetti. I like spaghetti.

Music as they return to the caravan. While Mr Twit prepares the table and lays cutlery, Mrs Twit puts spaghetti in a saucepan, then, unseen by Mr Twit, goes DS and finds some squirming worms. She smiles as she puts them in the saucepan. Mr Twit sits at the table, takes off his shoes, wriggles his toes and, leaning back, dozes off to sleep. As he snores, his beard lifts up and down. Mrs Twit returns smugly with the saucepan. Facing us she continues to prepare the meal, cooking then serving up the spaghetti and sprinkling cheese and sauce on top. Eventually she brings forward two plates of spaghetti. Mr Twit's is moving. Mrs Twit finds a dinner gong and, holding it very close to the sleeping Mr Twit's ear, bangs it very loudly. Mr Twit wakes with a start and nearly falls off his chair

Mrs Twit (*sweetly*) Your spaghetti, my dreamboat, my dove!
Mr Twit Mmm. Scrummy. (*He picks up his fork and goes to take some spaghetti*)

Meanwhile Mrs Twit tucks into hers

  Hey, my spaghetti is moving.
Mrs Twit What's that, my angel-puss?
Mr Twit It's all squirmy. (*He holds up the plate. It is heaving*)
Mrs Twit It's a new kind. It's called Squiggly Spaghetti. It's delicious. Eat it up while it's nice and hot.

Mr Twit starts to tuck in, forking up the spaghetti and shovelling it into his mouth, slurping and leaving a mess on his beard. Mrs Twit eagerly watches

Mr Twit (*chewing hard*) It's not as good as the ordinary kind. It's too squishy.
Mrs Twit Oh? I find it very tasty.
Mr Twit (*swallowing a mouthful*) I find it rather bitter. It's got a distinctly bitter flavour. Buy the other kind next time. (*But he goes on eating, with the occasional burp*)

Mrs Twit can hardly contain her delight. As he finishes his plateful...

Mrs Twit You want to know why your spaghetti was squirmy and squishy?
Mr Twit (*wiping his mouth on the tablecloth*) Why?
Mrs Twit And why it had a nasty bitter taste?
Mr Twit Why?
Mrs Twit Because it was *worms*! (*She roars with laughter*) Because it was WORMS!

Mr Twit reacts with sickly horror

  Music builds as Mr Twit roars at Mrs Twit and chases her round the table and off stage

*The Lighting fades. The music changes as the Lighting fades up on the cage.
It is morning. The monkeys wake up and stretch. The Narrator comes forward*

Narrator Next day, as the Muggle-Wump family woke up...

The Birds enter. They fly around

Little Muggle-Wump 1 Mum! Dad!
Little Muggle-Wump 2 Look!
Little Muggle-Wump 3 The birds are back!

The Birds settle on the tree

Narrator The birds had arrived earlier than usual. The day before they had
  been curious to see the Muggle-Wumps in their cage. They didn't like to
  see other creatures locked up, robbed of their freedom. They felt sorry for
  them.
Muggle-Wump (*calling*) Hallo, birds! Come on over!
Muggle-Wumps Come on! Come on!

The Birds fly over and land on the cage

Muggle-Wump Good morning!

The Birds twitter

Little Muggle-Wump 1 What are they saying, Dad?
Muggle-Wump Good morning, I suppose.
Mrs Muggle-Wump We can't understand their language.

The Birds twitter

Little Muggle-Wump 2 Why not, Mum?
Mrs Muggle-Wump They're English birds.
Little Muggle-Wump 3 Maybe they could help us go home.
Muggle-Wump How? They're only birds.

The Birds twitter

Little Muggle-Wump 1 The Roly-Poly Bird could help us.
Muggle-Wump He's in Africa.
Little Muggle-Wump 2 (*to the Birds*) Do you know the Roly-Poly Bird?
Little Muggle-Wump 3 He's our best friend.

Mrs Muggle-Wump Of course they don't.

Suddenly Mr Twit enters, wearing a trainer's hat

Muggle-Wump Shhh. Look out!
Mr Twit Come on, my lovelies. Training time!
Little Muggle-Wumps Oh, no.
Muggle-Wump Shhh.
Mr Twit (*seeing the Birds*) Clear off, you pesky birds. Don't want you messing my lovelies' cage. (*He waves Mrs Twit's stick and rattles the bars*)

The Birds fly off and return to the tree. They watch the ensuing training session. Mr Twit opens the cage door with the key. The Muggle-Wumps venture out, stretching their limbs

Out you come. (*He contains them in the "ring" with the stick*) Stay! Stay! Still. Now, listen, my lovelies. I've had a wheeze, a brilliant idea. Mr Twit's Miraculous Monkey Act needs to be different. Original. Unique. So from now on you will perform your tricks, wait for it, it's classic, you will perform your tricks … UPSIDE DOWN. The world's first Great Upside Down Monkey Circus!

The Muggle-Wumps look on, bemused, unable to understand

Look, like this, my lovelies. (*He tries to stand on his head. He falls over. He gets up*) Well, something like that. Right, come on then. Up and over. Up and over. On your hands!

Music as the Muggle-Wumps are forced into various positions. They attempt various acrobatic tricks with varying degrees of success. Mr Twit barks instructions. The instructions should not be too wordy. Phrases like: "Up! Down! Over! Stay! Arms out! Climb! Go!" Optional: Mrs Twit could come to watch for a while, occasionally contributing disparaging remarks like: "Rotten! Rubbishy! Ridiculous! Ropy! Bosh! Tosh! Bilge! Useless! Sad!" She should leave before the Muggle-Wumps achieve anything too impressive. After several different configurations, they all attempt a kind of upside down pyramid. This should be as impressive as possible

Hold it there. Stop wobbling! Yes! Yes! It's coming! It's coming! Well done, my lovelies. Down, down, back in the cage now. (*He allows them to stand again and forces them back into the cage*) Clever, clever. You deserve some breakfast, yes, you do. Bananas and monkey nuts, coming right up. Good monkeys. Good monkeys. (*He locks the cage door, pockets the key and starts to go back to the caravan*)

The Birds twitter. Mr Twit sees them

Clear off! When we want an audience, we'll invite one. Clear off! (*He brandishes the stick*)

The Birds fly up and exit

Mr Twit exits happily to the caravan

Narrator Mr Twit was happy with his monkeys' progress. His happiness was not shared by the Muggle-Wumps.

In the cage the Muggle-Wumps unwind

Little Muggle-Wump 1 I feel giddy.
Little Muggle-Wump 2 I feel dizzy.
Little Muggle-Wump 3 I feel sick.
Mrs Muggle-Wump Take deep breaths, children. (*To her husband*) Oh, Muggle-Wump, why does that horrid man make us do such stupid, undignified things?
Muggle-Wump I don't know, dear, but I *do* know that if we stay here much longer, the children will grow ill. They may even die.
Mrs Muggle-Wump Die?
Little Muggle-Wumps (*overhearing*) Die?
Mrs Muggle-Wump No, no, children. (*She thinks quickly*) Try.
Muggle-Wump Yes, try. We must all try to be brave, like the Roly-Poly Bird said when we...
Mrs Muggle-Wump ...when he said goodbye. Try to be brave. Yes?
Little Muggle-Wumps We'll try.

But they begin to sob

Muggle-Wump (*frustrated*) We've got to get out of this cage. (*He rattles the bars*)
Mrs Muggle-Wump But how?
Muggle-Wump (*with an idea*) The door! The man opens it with a special thing. He puts it in, turns it and the door opens.
Mrs Muggle-Wump What's it called? (*To the audience*) Does anyone know?
Audience Key!
Muggle-Wump A what?

Audience Key!
Mrs Muggle-Wump Thank you!
Muggle-Wump The key. (*Excitedly, to his family*) We'll steal the key.
Mrs Muggle-Wump But how?
Muggle-Wump I don't know yet, but...
Mrs Muggle-Wump (*having an idea; to the audience*) Will *you* help us?
Audience Yes!
Muggle-Wump You will?
Audience Yes!
Muggle-Wump Thank you. Now, when...

Mr and Mrs Twit enter from the caravan. Mrs Twit carries the food bowl

Narrator Look out, Muggle-Wumps!
Mrs Muggle-Wump Shh! They're coming!

The Muggle-Wumps settle

Mr Twit Don't forget. They're only allowed to eat upside down.
Mrs Twit All right, all right. Where's the key?

Mr Twit hands Mrs Twit the key, then returns to the caravan

Mr Twit (*turning*) Upside down!
Mrs Twit I know. Keep your hair on!

Mr Twit exits

Mrs Twit puts the key in the lock. Tension music

Right, come on, you ugly lot. Upside down or no breakfast. (*She opens the cage door, leaving the key in the lock. She enters the cage to put down the food bowl*) Up on your hands! Move! (*She prods them with the stick*)

Unseen by Mrs Twit, Muggle-Wump slips out of the cage, and deftly removes the key from the lock

Muggle-Wump (*whispering to the audience*) I've got it! (*He nips back inside*)
Mrs Twit Upside down, I said!

All the Muggle-Wumps manage to stand or crouch upside down

That's better. Now, eat. (*She emerges and closes the door*)

Before she has time to think about locking it, Mr Twit appears and shouts from the caravan

Mr Twit Are they upside down?
Mrs Twit (*moving towards Mr Twit*) Yes, yes.
Mr Twit All of them? Little ones too?
Mrs Twit Little ones too. See for yourself.

Mr Twit goes to the cage and looks

Mr Twit (*triumphantly*) Yes! Yes! (*He returns to the caravan, passing Mrs Twit*)

Mrs Twit returns to the cage. She reaches for the key, but it's not in the lock

Mrs Twit Funny. (*To herself*) Where's the key? (*She delves into a pocket*) Not there. (*She thinks. Then she tries to pull the door open*)

Muggle-Wump is holding it shut from inside

Mmm. It's locked all right. I must have locked it. (*To herself*) Then where's the key? (*She checks her pocket again*)
Muggle-Wump (*to the audience*) Please! If she asks, tell her she locked the door!
Mrs Twit (*seeing the audience and stepping* DS) 'Ere, you lot, did I lock that door?

If necessary, the Muggle-Wumps encourage the audience

Audience Yes.
Mrs Twit Are you sure?
Audience Yes.
Mrs Twit Did Mr Twit take the key?
Audience Yes.
Mrs Twit Are you sure?
Audience Yes.
Mrs Twit Oh. (*Suspiciously*) You're not having me on, are you?
Audience No.
Mrs Twit 'Cos if you are, you'll feel my big stick on your little bums, d'you hear? (*She brandishes her stick and probably gets booed as a result*)

Mrs Twit exits

In the cage, Muggle-Wump holds up the key

Muggle-Wump (*to the audience*) Thank you! (*To the other Muggle-Wumps*) I've got it! (*He holds up the key*) We fooled her!

Cheers. The Muggle-Wumps jump up and down with excitement

Come on, Muggle-Wumps! We're going home! (*He starts to carefully open the cage door and lead the others out*)

But suddenly Mr Twit enters, carrying a ladder

The audience possibly shout a warning. In any event...

Aaaaah! Back in! Back in!

The Muggle-Wumps scramble back and turn upside down. Muggle-Wump closes the cage door. Music as Mr Twit takes a quick look at the Muggle-Wumps to check they are upside down, then heads for the tree. As he leans the ladder against the tree, the Narrator steps forward

Narrator Mr Twit now turned his evil attentions towards ... the birds.

Mr Twit returns briefly to the caravan

His twisted, nasty, cruel mind had come up with another twisted, nasty, cruel idea.

Mr Twit comes back carrying a large pot marked "Hugtight Glue"

This time the birds would meet their match. This time there would be no escape...

Mr Twit climbs the ladder and, using a large paintbrush, coats the top of the branches of the tree with "Hugtight Glue". Hopefully the glue makes the branches glisten. Music echoes Mr Twit's evil words

Mr Twit   Coat ev'ry branch with Hugtight Glue
                               Birds, I've a big surprise for you!
                               Slop it and slap it and spread it along
                               Soon you'll sing your final song!
                               Land on the tree
                               And you'll never get free!
                               Tough titties, hard luck
                               You'll be stuck, stuck, stuck!
                               So stand by, birds, for a great big fright,

Stand by, Twits, it's Bird Pie night!

Laughing maniacally, Mr Twit climbs down and carries the ladder and the pot of glue back to behind the caravan

The music changes to build the tension. Muggle-Wump opens the cage door and the Muggle-Wumps all creep softly out

Muggle-Wump Come on! We're free! We're free!

As they reach the centre of the "ring" they are stopped in their tracks by a terrifying sound, a gale-force wind accompanied by a loud flapping noise. The Muggle-Wumps start to panic as exciting lighting effects heighten the drama

Mrs Muggle-Wump What's happening?
Little Muggle-Wumps Help! Help!
Muggle-Wump It must be a storm!

The Muggle-Wumps, arms flailing, dash to and fro, bumping into each other. As the sound effects intensify, they all look to Muggle-Wump for guidance

(*Shouting*) Take shelter in the tree!
Mrs Muggle-Wump (*shouting*) In the tree? Are you sure?
Muggle-Wump (*shouting*) We'll be safe there! To … the … tree!

Mrs Muggle-Wump nods her agreement. Hopefully the audience realize the tree is not a safe place in which to take shelter

Muggle-Wump | (*to Little Muggle-Wumps; together*) Climb … the
Mrs Muggle-Wump | … tree!

Immediately, the Lighting changes to a strobe or similar effect. The branches glow and pulsate. In slow motion, the Muggle-Wumps head for the tree. Hopefully, the audience, knowing the tree is coated with glue, shout out a warning. The tension and audience participation build toward a climax as the Muggle-Wumps get nearer and nearer the tree

Suddenly, Black-out

CURTAIN

Live or recorded music plays during the interval

ACT II

As the House Lights fade, an entr'acte, similar to the earlier overture, is played. Fanfare/drumroll

The Narrator steps forward

Narrator Ladies and gentlemen, young ladies and gentlemen, welcome back to the second half of our exciting, extraordinary extravaganza entittle-i-titled (*he encourages the audience to join in*) ... *The Twits!* Please welcome back the magnificent Muggle-Wumps!

Musical chord as the Muggle-Wumps enter with a flourish, then take their places by the cage

You will recall that in the nail-biting climax to the first half, the Muggle-Wumps had just escaped from the cage, when, suddenly...

As the Muggle-Wumps reach the centre of the "ring", in a reprise of the end of Act I, they are stopped in their tracks by the terrifying wind and flapping noise. They start to panic as exciting Lighting effects again heighten the drama

Mrs Muggle-Wump What's happening?
Little Muggle-Wumps Help! Help!
Muggle-Wump It must be a storm!

The Muggle-Wumps, arms flailing, dash to and fro, bumping into each other. As the sound effects intensify, they all look to Muggle-Wump for guidance

(*Shouting*) Take shelter in the tree!
Mrs Muggle-Wump (*shouting*) In the tree? Are you sure?
Muggle-Wump (*shouting*) We'll be safe there! To ... the ... tree!

Mrs Muggle-Wump nods her agreement

Muggle-Wump } (*to Little Muggle-Wumps; together*) Climb ... the
Mrs Muggle-Wump | ... tree!

The Lighting changes to a strobe or similar effect. The branches glow and pulsate. In slow motion the Muggle-Wumps head for the glue-coated tree. Hopefully the audience shout out a warning. The tension and audience participation build towards a climax as the Muggle-Wumps get nearer and nearer the tree. Suddenly the lighting and sound effects stop. The Little Muggle-Wumps look up and point to the sky

Little Muggle-Wump 1 Mum!
Little Muggle-Wump 2 Dad!
Little Muggle-Wump 3 Look!
All Muggle-Wumps (*looking up*) It's the Roly-Poly Bird!
Muggle-Wump It wasn't a storm. It was the Roly-Poly Bird!

Music and bright Lighting as the Roly-Poly Bird flies joyfully in

The Muggle-Wumps cheer

Roly-Poly Bird Hallo, Muggle-Wump! Hallo, Mrs Muggle-Wump! Hallo, little Muggle-Wumps!
Muggle-Wumps Hallo, Roly-Poly Bird!
Muggle-Wump You've come!
Roly-Poly Bird Of course. I promised I would! And the Roly-Poly Bird never breaks a promise. I promised I would come!
Mrs Muggle-Wump But not till the spring.
Roly-Poly Bird I was worried about you. I came early.
Mrs Muggle-Wump Thank you.
Roly-Poly Bird Have you been brave? Are your tails up? Are your heads held high?
Muggle-Wump Of course.
Mrs Muggle-Wump We're free!
Roly-Poly Bird Why are you dressed in those silly, degrading clothes?
Muggle-Wump They made us.
Roly-Poly Bird They? Who are *they*? (*He sees the audience, with a gasp*) Them?
Muggle-Wump No, no. These are our friends. They helped us escape.
Roly-Poly Bird Escape?
Mrs Muggle-Wump From that cage. They locked us in.
Roly-Poly Bird (*indicating the audience*) *They* did?
Muggle-Wump No!
Roly-Poly Bird (*to the audience*) Then *who* did?
Audience The Twits!
Roly-Poly Bird Who?
Audience The Twits!

Roly-Poly Bird The Twits?

Muggle-Wump Yes. They made us perform tricks.

Little Muggle-Wumps Upside down!

Roly-Poly Bird Upside down? Unnatural! Outrageous! These Twits must be taught a lesson. (*To the audience*) Mustn't they?

Audience Yes!

Muggle-Wump But we can't stay here.

Mrs Muggle-Wump The Twits might catch us again.

Roly-Poly Bird I see. Let me think, let me think, let me think! (*He has an idea*) Ah! Inspiration! Quick, Muggle-Wumps, climb up that tree. We can plan in safety there.

The Muggle-Wumps and the Roly-Poly Bird head for the tree. The audience hopefully react

Audience No!

The Muggle-Wumps and the Roly-Poly Bird stop

Roly-Poly Bird (*to the audience*) Why not?

Audience There's glue on the tree!

Roly-Poly Bird Glue? (*He carefully moves or flies to the tree. He looks and sniffs. To the Muggle-Wumps*) Your friends are right. Glue.

Muggle-Wump What's glue?

Roly-Poly Bird Horrid sticky stuff. (*To the audience*) Who put it there?

Audience The Twits.

Roly-Poly Bird Why?

Audience To catch the birds.

Roly-Poly Bird (*horrified*) To catch the birds!

Muggle-Wump We know them. They often perch there.

Roly-Poly Bird (*to the audience*) But why should the Twits want to catch them?

Audience To eat them / To make a Bird Pie.

Roly-Poly Bird (*even more horrified*) To eat them in a Bird Pie?

Audience Yes.

Roly-Poly Bird Barbarous! Brutal! Beastly!

Muggle-Wump The birds may fly back soon.

Mrs Muggle-Wump We must warn them!

Roly-Poly Bird Indeed we must.

Muggle-Wump But they don't understand us!

Roly-Poly Bird They'll understand me! I'm a bird too. (*He takes in the audience*) And our friends will help. Won't you?

Audience Yes.

The Muggle-Wumps react happily

Roly-Poly Bird Excellent. Now, let me think, let me think, let me think. (*Suddenly*) Ah! Inspiration!
> When the birds are very near
> Near enough for them to hear
> We'll shout this rhyme—loud and clear...

Pause, as the Roly-Poly Bird concentrates

> There's sticky stick stuff all over the tree!
> If you land in the branches, you'll never get free!
> So fly away! Fly away! Stay up high!
> Or you'll finish up tonight in a hot Bird Pie!

Got it? Now, everybody...
> There's sticky stick stuff all over...

(*He meanders to a halt, because the participation is limited*) Where were you? Where were you?

Muggle-Wump We need to learn it first, Roly-Poly Bird.

Roly-Poly Bird Of course! After me...
> There's sticky stick stuff all over the tree!

The audience joins in with them all

All There's sticky stick stuff all over the tree!
Roly-Poly Bird If you land in the branches, you'll never get free!
All If you land in the branches, you'll never get free!
Roly-Poly Bird So fly away! Fly away! Stay up high!
All So fly away! Fly away! Stay up high!
Roly-Poly Bird Or you'll finish up tonight in a hot Bird Pie!
All Or you'll finish up tonight in a hot Bird Pie!

Roly-Poly Bird Good! Let's put it all together. And listen, to make sure we all say it at the same time, I'll give a signal. (*He thinks*) How about this? (*He makes a loud piercing whistle*) Yes? Ready, then. Good and loud! Wait for the signal. (*He whistles*)

All There's sticky stick stuff all over the tree!
> If you land in the branches, you'll never get free!
> So fly away! Fly away! Stay up high!
> Or you'll finish up tonight in a hot Bird Pie!

Roly-Poly Bird Excellent. Thank you!

The Muggle-Wumps cheer and jump about with excitement. Suddenly they hear a loud voice

Mr Twit (*off; loudly*) Hurry up! Get a move on!

There is an instant change of mood. The Muggle-Wumps tremble and dither

Little Muggle-Wump 1 (*quickly*) Mum!
Little Muggle-Wump 2 (*quickly*) Dad!
Little Muggle-Wump 3 It's them!
Muggle-Wump ⎱ (*together*) The Twits!
Mrs Muggle-Wump ⎰
Roly-Poly Bird (*taking control*) Quick! Back in the cage!

The Muggle-Wumps hurry back inside the cage, closing the door, then standing or crouching upside down. The Roly-Poly Bird positions himself out of sight of the Twits, but in view of the audience. Ideally he should "fly" up above the action

Mr Twit enters from the caravan

Mr Twit (*shouting*) Come on, you dozy doughnut, shift yourself!

Mrs Twit enters with a large stoneware bowl marked "Bird Pie"

Mrs Twit Pipe down, you hairy great turnip. I'm behind you.
Mr Twit You don't want to miss all the fun.
Mrs Twit So long as it works. (*She see the Muggle-Wumps and prods through the cage bars with her walking stick*) Get up! Get up!

The Muggle-Wumps shuffle about

Mr Twit Of course it'll work. Can't fail. We'll stand over here and watch.

The Twits lurk in the shadows

So stand by, birds, for a great big fright.
Mr Twit ⎱ (*together*) Stand by, Twits, it's Bird Pie night!
Mrs Twit ⎰

They cackle in evil anticipation

Mr Twit (*pointing up*) They're coming! They're coming!
Mrs Twit Shhh.

They watch

Music as the Birds enter. They fly around for a circuit or two. Then they hover above the tree. The Roly-Poly Bird whistles

All Except The Twits There's sticky stick stuff all over the tree!
If you land in the branches, you'll never get free!
So fly away! Fly away! Stay up high!
Or you'll finish up tonight in a hot Bird Pie!

Music as the Birds retreat. They fly up and away from the tree and land safely on the cage. The Twits emerge. The Roly-Poly Bird, the Muggle-Wumps and the audience cheer

Mr Twit No! Over there! You're meant to be on the tree over there!

The Birds twitter, bobbing cockily up and down on the cage

Mrs Twit Typical! You silly, great twit, you're useless!

Mrs Twit storms back to the caravan with her Bird Pie bowl

Mr Twit (*furious in defeat*) Oooooh! It's not fair!

The birds twitter, the Muggle-Wumps chatter. Hopefully the audience laugh

It's not funny! (*To the Muggle-Wumps*) Shut up! (*To the audience*) Shut up!

Eventually

Right, that's it! (*He scares off the Birds with a huge gesture*)

The Birds fly away and exit

Mr Twit dashes back to the caravan

The Narrator comes forward

Narrator Mr Twit was not a man to be laughed at. He was not a man to be easily beaten.

Mr Twit enters with a ladder and a glue pot. He leans the ladder against the cage

Bird Pie he wanted. And Bird Pie he was determined to have.

Music as Mr Twit climbs the ladder and paints the top of the cage with glue. The Muggle-Wumps cower below, not wanting to be splattered with glue. This glue painting could be performed speeded up, like a silent film, with appropriate musical accompaniment. Mr Twit climbs down

Mr Twit (*challengingly*) Now I'll get you! Whichever one you sit on!

Mr Twit cackles, collects the ladder and exits behind the caravan

Roly-Poly Bird All clear!

The Muggle-Wumps come out of the cage, stretching their limbs. The Roly-Poly Bird flies down to meet them

Muggle-Wump (*to the audience*) Thank you, everyone, you saved the birds!
Roly-Poly Bird But not for long, Muggle-Wump. We must warn them again. Let me think, let me think, let me think! (*He pauses for thought*) Ah! Inspiration! After me, everyone...
There's sticky stuff now on the cage *and* the tree!

The audience joins in with them all

All	There's sticky stuff now on the cage *and* the tree!
Roly-Poly Bird	If you land on the cage, you'll never get free!
All	If you land on the cage, you'll never get free!
Roly-Poly Bird	So fly away! Fly away! Stay up high!
All	So fly away! Fly away! Stay up high!
Roly-Poly Bird	Or you'll finish up tonight in a hot Bird Pie!
All	Or you'll finish up tonight in a hot Bird Pie!

Roly-Poly Bird Excellent. Let's put it all together. After the signal. (*He whistles*)
All There's sticky stuff now on the cage *and* the tree!
If you land on the cage, you'll never get free!
So fly away! Fly away! Stay up high!
Or you'll finish up tonight in a hot Bird Pie!
Roly-Poly Bird Thank you. Good luck!
Mr Twit (*off*) Come on!
Muggle-Wump Quick!

The Muggle-Wumps hurry back into the cage, standing or crouching upside down. The Roly-Poly Bird moves away

Mr and Mrs Twit enter, carrying the Bird Pie bowl

Mrs Twit (*sceptically*) Here we go again.
Mr Twit This time, my luscious little humbug, we cannot fail!

They position themselves, crouching DC, *with their backs to the audience*

                          Stand by, birds, for a great big fright.
Mr Twit ⎫
Mrs Twit ⎭ (*together*) Stand by, Twits, it's Bird Pie night!

   *Music as the Birds enter. They circle, then hover above the tree, then swoop
   up and over to the cage*

The Roly-Poly Bird whistles

All Except The Twits There's sticky stuff now on the cage *and* the tree!
                          If you land on the cage, you'll never get free!
                          So fly away! Fly away! Stay up high!
                          Or you'll finish up tonight in a hot Bird Pie!

*Music as the Birds react. They fly up and away from the cage. They fly safely
over to the caravan and land on the roof*

Mr Twit No! No! Aaaaah! It's not fair!

The Birds twitter, the Muggle-Wumps chatter, the audience hopefully laugh

   It's not funny!

More laughter

Mrs Twit It's not funny. It's pathetic. Bird Pie? No chance.
Mr Twit (*suddenly realizing, noticing the audience*) It was them!
Mrs Twit What?
Mr Twit Warning the birds. It was *them*. (*To the audience*) You smarmy
   little goody goodies!
Mrs Twit (*to the audience*) You sneaky little sissies!
Mr Twit You squealing little blabbers, you blabbing little squealers!
Mrs Twit You'll pay for that!
Mr Twit Through the toes!
Mrs Twit Nose!
Mr Twit (*thinking Mrs Twit said "No"*) Yes!
Mrs Twit Nose!
Mr Twit Yes!

Mrs Twit Oh, never mind.

Mr Twit (*to the audience*) If you make one squeak next time, I'll glue you to your seats!

Mrs Twit Next time? What do you mean, next time?

Mr Twit Third time lucky! (*He remembers the birds are on the roof and therefore talks in a loud whisper*) I'll glue the roof!

Mrs Twit (*also speaking in a loud whisper*) Roof? What roof?

Mr Twit The roof of the caravan.

Mrs Twit (*shouting*) Over my dead body!

Mr Twit Shhh.

Mrs Twit (*in a loud whisper*) Over my dead body. I'm not having you smearing sticky glue all over the roof of our caravan. (*She threatens him with her stick*)

Mr Twit (*a frustrated shout of rage*) Ooooooh! (*He runs towards the caravan, shaking his fists at the birds*)

The Birds fly up a little, then back on to the roof, twittering

I'll wipe that silly laugh off your beaks! I'll get you, you feathery frumps! I'll wring your necks, the whole lot of you. I'll have you bubbling in the Bird Pie pot before this day is out!

Mrs Twit Huh! Promises, promises.

Mr Twit strives to think of an idea. Suddenly...

Mr Twit I've got it! A great idea.

Music echoes his evil plan

We'll both go into town right away and we'll each buy ... a gun! How's that?

Mrs Twit Brilliant! We'll buy those big shotguns that spray out fifty bullets or more with each bang!

Mr Twit Perfect!

He notices the Muggle-Wumps, who are no longer upside down, but standing watching. Mr Twit approaches the cage

And you lot. Upside down and jump to it. One on top of the other!

Mrs Twit (*joining him*) Quick! Get on with it or you'll feel my stick!

The Muggle-Wumps struggle back into upside down positions

Mr Twit Now stay there till we come back.

Mr and Mrs Twit exit

Pause

The Roly-Poly Bird, from above, checks the Twits have gone

Roly-Poly Bird All clear!

The Muggle-Wumps stand upright and come out of the cage. The Narrator comes forward

Narrator With the Twits out of the way for a while, the Roly-Poly Bird
    announced...
Roly-Poly Bird It is time for a conference!
Little Muggle-Wump 1 What's a conference?
Muggle-Wump A meeting.
Narrator Everyone was invited. The Muggle-Wumps!

Music as the Muggle-Wumps gather

    The birds!

Music as the Birds fly from the roof and perch on the "ring"

    And the Roly-Poly Bird himself!

Music as the Roly-Poly Bird flies in to "take the chair"

    Many subjects were discussed.

Music as all animatedly mime discussion. Then...

Roly-Poly Bird Freedom for Muggle-Wumps!
Muggle-Wump Protection for the birds!
Mrs Muggle-Wump ⎫ (*together*) Down with the Twits!
Little Muggle-Wumps ⎭

*The Birds do a twittering echo of "Down with the Twits". The mimed
discussion continues*

Narrator It was agreed that...
All Down with the Twits!
Narrator ...should be their first target. If the Twits could be defeated, the
    Muggle-Wumps would be free and the birds would be safe.

All Down with the Twits!
Roly-Poly Bird But how?

Music accompanies more animated mimed "discussion". Then...

Muggle-Wump Teach them a lesson!
Mrs Muggle-Wump Lock them in the cage!
Roly-Poly Bird Glue them to the roof!

*In the original production, three of the children operating the Bird puppets
also took lines:*

> **Bird 1** Peck their eyes out!
> **Bird 2** Make Twit Pie!
> **Bird 3** Give them a bath!

Little Muggle-Wump 1 Prod them with a stick!
Little Muggle-Wump 2 Make them do tricks!
Little Muggle-Wump 3 Turn them upside down!

A pause. A gasp

Roly-Poly Bird What was that?
Little Muggle-Wump 3 Turn them upside down.

All react delighted

All Turn them upside down!
Narrator Everyone set to work!

*Music. A flurry of activity. Strobe lighting perhaps. The idea of the sequence
is that all the animals and birds make the caravan interior look upside down
by glueing the carpet and the furniture to the ceiling. How much of the activity
can be in view of the audience is really up to the set designer. But ideally the
inside of the caravan should be made to revolve, thus creating the illusion of
an upside down room. During the sequence, perhaps we see the Roly-Poly
Bird supervising operations, the Muggle-Wumps, led by Muggle-Wump,
finding the glue pot and paintbrush and entering the caravan, and the Birds
zooming about above and behind the caravan. It may be possible to see the
Muggle-Wumps painting the ceiling with glue. It may be possible to see some
furniture being removed, turned upside down and stuck on the ceiling—
whatever is theatrically practical. The sequence might best be performed as
a choreographed routine*

The following accompanying narration by the Narrator is optional

The Muggle-Wumps found Mr Twit's pot of glue and lots of paintbrushes. Then everyone smeared and slapped the sticky glue all over the Twits' ceiling. The birds joined in. Buzzards, magpies, rooks, ravens, and many more. Then, in one mighty pull, they dragged the carpet from under the furniture and hoisted it up on to the ceiling. And there it stuck! Next, the table and chairs, the sofa, the sideboard, the lamps, the ornaments, *everything* was turned upside down, glue brushed on the bottom and then stuck on the carpeted ceiling. And finally the pictures on the wall were upturned too. Now the Twits' room was completely and utterly *upside down*!

After the choreographed sequence and, if used, the optional narration, the final revelation, accompanied by exciting music, is made. The room is revolved and the upside down caravan interior revealed to the audience. The Birds twitter on the roof, the Muggle-Wumps chatter, and hopefully the audience cheer. The Roly-Poly Bird surveys the scene

Roly-Poly Bird Expertly done! Congratulations one and all!
Muggle-Wump When the Twits go in, they'll think they're upside down, the maggoty old monsters!
Roly-Poly Bird But wait. Their room is upside down, you Muggle-Wumps will be upside down. But what about the birds?

Music as the Birds fly up, turn over, then land and lie on the roof upside down. The Muggle-Wumps chatter and clap

Muggle-Wump Yes! (*A sudden realization*) But what about (*he indicates the audience*) our friends?
Mrs Muggle-Wump *They're* not upside down.

All look concerned

Roly-Poly Bird Let me think, let me think, let me think! (*He pauses for thought*) Ah! Inspiration! (*To the audience*) Everybody. Please help fool the Twits. Take off your shoes! Yes, quickly, please. Take off your shoes.

The audience are encouraged further, if necessary, to remove their shoes

Now put your shoes on your hands. And stretch your arms up above your heads!

The Muggle-Wumps mime a demonstration

Yes, yes! Now, hold them still and lower your heads a little! Yes, yes!
Muggle-Wump You look upside down!
Mrs Muggle-Wump You really do!

Suddenly...

Mr Twit ⎱ (*off; together*) Stand by, birds, for a great big fright...
Mrs Twit ⎰
Little Muggle-Wumps They're coming! They're coming!

The Muggle-Wumps dash back to the cage and position themselves

Roly-Poly Bird (*to the audience*) Arms down, everyone, but shoes on hands
 ready. Wait for my signal!
Mr Twit ⎱ (*together*) Stand by, Twits, it's Bird Pie night!
Mrs Twit ⎰

*They can repeat their rhyme if necessary. The Roly-Poly Bird flies out of the
way but still in vision. A musical pulse for tension*

 Mr and Mrs Twit enter, carrying big shotguns

Mr Twit I'm glad to see those monkeys are still upside down.
Mrs Twit They're too stupid to do anything else. Hey, look, those cheeky
 birds are still on the roof.
Mr Twit Let's blast them with our lovely new guns!

They start to aim

Mrs Twit Hang on! Why aren't they moving?
Mr Twit Are they dead already?

Music and the birds flutter, rise a little, still upside down, then drop to the roof

Mr Twit ⎱ (*together*) Aah! They're not dead ... they're upside down! They
Mrs Twit ⎰   can't be. They *are*!

They stand bemused

 *Music as two Birds enter, carrying paint brushes in their beaks. Each
 swoops down and brushes the tops of Mr and Mrs Twits' heads*

Mr Twit ⎱ (*together*) What was that?
Mrs Twit ⎰

They look up to see the Birds swoop up and fly off

Mrs Twit Ugh! That beastly bird has dropped his dirty droppings on my head!

Mr Twit On mine too! I felt it. I felt it! Ugh!

Mrs Twit Don't touch it! You'll get it all over your hands! Come inside and we'll wash it off.

Mr Twit (*looking up*) Filthy, dirty brutes! I'll bet they did it on purpose. (*He brandishes his shotgun*) Just you wait! Grrrrh!

The Twits go to the caravan. Lights up on the upside-down room. The Twits stop and stand aghast

Mrs Twit (*gasping*) What's this?

Mr Twit What's happened?

Mrs Twit Look! That's the floor! The floor's up there! This is the ceiling! We're standing on the ceiling!

Mr Twit We're upside down! We *must* be upside down. We're standing on the ceiling looking down at the floor!

Mrs Twit Help! Help! I'm beginning to feel giddy! (*She totters*)

Mr Twit (*trying to convince himself*) Wait. We *can't* be upside down.

Mrs Twit We are! We are!

Mr Twit If *we're* upside down, the monkeys would have looked the right way up. But they didn't.

Mrs Twit Let's look again.

As they return towards the cage, the Muggle-Wumps all reverse themselves, standing upright, balancing on one another. The Twits arrive

Mr Twit ⎫
                  (*together*) Aaaaah! They're the right way up!
Mrs Twit ⎭

Mr Twit It can't be true!

Mrs Twit It *is* true!

Mr Twit What about (*he indicates the audience, but not looking at them*) those smarmy little goody goodies?

Mrs Twit What about them?

Mr Twit They're the right way up. But if *we're* upside down, *they'd look* upside down.

Mrs Twit (*confused*) Er ... yes.

Mr Twit Let's have a look.

As they turn to move towards the audience, the Roly-Poly Bird whistles. The audience hold up their arms, with their shoes on their hands. The Twits arrive DS

Mr Twit ⎫ (*seeing the audience; together*) Aaah! They're upside down!
Mrs Twit ⎭
Mr Twit It can't be true!
Mrs Twit It *is* true!
Mr Twit ⎫ (*together*) Aaaaaaah!
Mrs Twit ⎭

They stagger back to the caravan

Roly-Poly Bird (*to the audience*) Thank you! It worked! Arms down!

The audience drop their arms. The Twits arrive in their upside down room

Mrs Twit (*in a panic*) We're upside down and all the blood's going to my head! If we don't do something quickly, I shall die, I know I will!
Mr Twit I've got it! We'll stand on our heads, then we'll be the right way up again!

Music as Mr and Mrs Twit stand on their heads. The Muggle-Wumps creep out of the cage to watch. The Birds fly up, right themselves and swoop down to watch. The Roly-Poly Bird goes nearer too. The Narrator comes forward

Narrator When the tops of their heads touched the floor, the sticky glue that the ravens had brushed on a few moments before did its job. The Twits were pinned down, cemented, glued, fixed to the floorboards.

The Twits strive unsuccessfully to get up

The Twits were well and truly stuck!

Hopefully the audience cheer, along with the Muggle-Wumps, the Roly-Poly Bird and the birds. The Lighting fades down on the caravan

The birds were safe!

Cheers

The Muggle-Wumps were free!

Music. The Muggle-Wumps remove their circus costumes and throw them in the cage

Muggle-Wump Thank you, Roly-Poly Bird.
Roly-Poly Bird Everybody helped. (*He indicates the audience*)

Muggle-Wumps (*to the audience*) Thank you!
Little Muggle-Wump 1 Mum!
Little Muggle-Wump 2 Dad!
Little Muggle-Wump 3 Can we go home now?
Mrs Muggle-Wump Can we go home, Roly-Poly Bird?
Roly-Poly Bird You most certainly can! I shall be proud to personally escort you! Goodbye, birds!
Muggle-Wumps Goodbye, birds!

The Birds twitter

Come, Muggle-Wumps!
Mrs Muggle-Wump Hold on tight!

The Muggle-Wumps all hold hands. Muggle-Wump holds on to the Roly-Poly Bird, who prepares for take off

Music and a sound effect as the Roly-Poly Bird and the Muggle-Wumps exit

The Birds watch

As the music swells, a puppet/cut-out of the Roly-Poly Bird and the Muggle-Wumps crosses the stage and exits

Then another, smaller, puppet flies across the other way. Finally an even smaller puppet crosses the stage. The Birds swoop and circle, then exit in formation in the other direction

The Narrator steps forward

Narrator After a few deservedly uncomfortable days, the Twits managed to struggle free.

The Twits enter, both with big bald patches on the tops of their heads. Mrs Twit, thanks to her nasty experience, is hunched up and stooping

Soon even they realized it was the room that was upside down, not them. They blamed each other for their stupid mistake, but never found out who had played such a clever trick on them.

The Twits go to the cage

They were furious that the monkeys had escaped.

The Twits Aaaaaah!

They turn towards the caravan. The roof is birdless

Narrator And that Bird Pie would never be on the menu.
The Twits Aaaaaah!
Narrator Now they had nothing left to do but the one thing they were best at—being nasty to one another.

The Twits turn and stand in the "ring"

Mr Twit You look all squashed down, my hunchy dumpling.
Mrs Twit I *feel* all squashed down, you whiskery old walrus. It's your fault. You said to stand on our heads!
Mr Twit I reckon as you're developing "the dreaded shrinks".
Mrs Twit No! Not "the dreaded shrinks"!
Mr Twit I reckon. Your head shrinks into your body. Then your body shrinks into your legs. Then your legs shrink into your feet. Then there's nothing left except a pair of old shoes and a bundle of old clothes.
Mrs Twit I can't bear it!
Mr Twit It's a terrible disease. The worst in the world.
Mrs Twit But isn't there anything we can do?
Mr Twit There's only one cure for "the dreaded shrinks".
Mrs Twit Tell me!
Mr Twit You must be stretched!

Music. Mr Twit fetches the bunches of helium balloons decorating the sides of the set. He attaches them to Mrs Twit. As more and more balloons are added, her body starts to straighten up

Can you feel the balloons stretching you?
Mrs Twit I can! I can!

A few more balloons are added. Mrs Twit starts to rise up in the air. Mr Twit holds on to her ankles

Aaaaah! Oooooh!

Mr Twit looks pleased with himself

You are holding on to me, aren't you? If you were to let go, who knows what might happen!

A musical sting as Mr Twit gets a nasty idea

Mr Twit Fear not, beloved! I'll never let you go!
Mrs Twit There's enough pull here to take me to the moon!
Mr Twit To the moon, my angel? What a thought! (*He lets go of her ankles*)

Mrs Twit begins to rise

Mrs Twit Oooh! Aaaah! Help!
Mr Twit Goodbye, you old hag! Goodbye for ever!

Mrs Twit rises higher. And higher. Mr Twit freezes, waving goodbye. The Narrator steps in

Narrator But we can't end our story like this! No, ladies and gentlemen, young ladies and gentlemen. That wouldn't be fair! Mr and Mrs Twit are as nasty as each other. They deserve each other. Mr Twit cannot be allowed to win! Bring on the birds!

Music as the Birds fly on and circle

Then, in the nick of time, they fly up and, with their beaks, begin to burst the balloons. Slowly, gracefully, Mrs Twit descends. She lands right on top of Mr Twit, who unfreezes to find himself up his wife's skirts. He circles, carrying her on his shoulders. Then they collapse in a heap. They struggle up, and Mrs Twit turns on Mr Twit

Mrs Twit You nasty ... loathsome ... horrible ... rotten ... stinking ... monstrous... Twit! I'll get you! You'll pay for that! I'll make you suffer! Come back! Come back!

Music as Mr Twit, terrified, makes his escape—possibly through the auditorium—chased by Mrs Twit. As they go; not all the insults are necessary, but enough to cover the exit

Mr Twit You frazzled old faggot!
Mrs Twit You grizzly old grunion!
Mr Twit You frumptious old freak!
Mrs Twit You troggy old turnip!
Mr Twit You maggoty old monkfish!
Mrs Twit You filthy old frumpet!
Mr Twit You mangy old mongoose!
Mrs Twit You whiskery old warthog!
Mr Twit I'll swish you to a swazzle!
Mrs Twit I'll swash you to a swizzle!

Mr Twit I'll gnash you to a gnozzle!
Mrs Twit I'll gnosh you to a gnazzle!

The Narrator returns

Narrator A fair ending, if not a happy one! But every story needs a truly happy ending, and this is no exception. Come with me, back to the green and pleasant rainforests of Africa!

Music as the scene changes back to the rainforest. Ropes, like vines, drop

The Muggle-Wumps, and the optional other monkeys, enter

They play happily on the ropes

The Muggle-Wumps are home!

In flies the Roly-Poly Bird

Roly-Poly Bird Wheeee! Morning, Muggle-Wumps!
Muggle-Wumps Morning, Roly-Poly Bird!
Roly-Poly Bird What a marvellous, magical morning!
Narrator And sometimes they enjoy performing in their own special monkey circus—but not, most definitely not, an upside down one. Ladies and gents, young ladies, young gents, put your hands together for the Roly-Poly Bird and the magnificent, *free*, Muggle-Wumps!

Music as the Muggle-Wumps and the Roly-Poly Bird perform a brief, exhilarating acrobatic routine, showing off their skills and celebrating their freedom. NB: in the original production, the Roly-Poly Bird entered after the Narrator's final speech, and her spoken exchange with the Muggle-Wumps was transposed accordingly

CURTAIN

FURNITURE AND PROPERTY LIST

Further dressing may be added at director's discretion

ACT I

On stage: **TWITS'** CARAVAN:
Carpet
Chairs
Table
Sofa
Sideboard
Lamps
Ornaments
Pictures
2 glasses of beer
Enormous joke mallet
Tutus or bolero jackets and hats for **Muggle-Wumps**
Glass of water
Cutlery
Spaghetti
Saucepan
Worms
Moving spaghetti
Cheese
Sauce
Plates
Dinner gong

Off stage: Large net on long pole (**Twits**)
Ropes like vines (**SM**)
Banana (**Mr Twit**)
Large net (**Mr Twit**)
Large cage (**Twits**)
Large key (**Mr Twit**)
Tree (**SM**)
Bowl of food (**Twits**)
Ladder (**Mr Twit**)
Large pot marked "Hugtight Glue", large paintbrush (**Mr Twit**)

Personal: **Mrs Twit:** walking stick
            Mr Twit: false teeth
            Mr Twit: piece of maggoty green cheese
            Mr Twit: mouldy old cornflake
            Mr Twit: slimy tail of tinned sardine
            Mrs Twit: glass eye
            Mr Twit: explorer's hat
            Mr Twit: large slimy frog
            Mr Twit: trainer's hat

ACT II

On stage: Glue pot
           Paintbrush
           Helium balloons

Off stage: Large stoneware bowl marked "Bird Pie" (**Mrs Twit**)
           Walking stick (**Mrs Twit**)
           Ladder, glue pot (**Mr Twit**)
           Big shotguns (**Twits**)
           Paint brushes (**Birds**)
           Ropes (**SM**)

LIGHTING PLOT

Property fittings required: nil
A circus ring with three additional settings: a caravan, a cage, a tree. The same
throughout

ACT I

EFFECTS PLOT

ACT I

Cue 1   To open Act I   (Page 1)
Jolly circus-style music, live or recorded (optional)

Cue 2   **Muggle-Wumps** reach centre of "ring"   (Page 22)
Bring up sound of gale-force wind and loud flapping noise

Cue 3   **Muggle-Wumps** dash to and fro   (Page 22)
Intensify sound effects

ACT II

Cue 4   **Muggle-Wumps** reach centre of "ring"   (Page 23)
Bring up sound of gale-force wind and loud flapping noise

Cue 5   **Muggle-Wumps** dash to and fro   (Page 23)
Intensify sound effects

Cue 6   **Muggle-Wumps** get nearer and nearer the tree   (Page 24)
Cut sound effects

Cue 7   **Muggle-Wumps** and **Roly-Poly Bird** exit   (Page 38)
Sound effect

THE LEARNING CENTRES
TOWN CENTRE CAMPUS
EASTWOOD LANE
ROTHERHAM S65 1EG

MADE AND PRINTED IN GREAT BRITAIN BY
LATIMER TREND & COMPANY LTD PLYMOUTH
MADE IN ENGLAND